A STROKE OF LUCK

A One Act Black Comedy

Will Butters

Published by Playstage
United Kingdom

An imprint of Write Publications Ltd

www.playsforadults.com

Designed by Kate Lowe, Greensands Graphics
Printed by Creeds Ltd, Bridport, Dorset

Note to producers staging "A Stroke of Luck"

The major challenge of this play is obviously for the actor recreating BILLY's stroke. The playwright hasn't made it easy because the stroke takes place during a scene that borders on farce and it is necessary to achieve a fine balance between comedy and tragedy. Fortunately, the script perfectly highlights the self-obsession and, at times, difficult behaviour of the character BILLY before the actual stroke occurs, so the audience has been 'set up', as it were, by the comedy and the interplay of the characters in the opening scene.

Once the stroke has happened, the responsibility for maintaining the comedy comes in the form of the three patients, SANDRA, HILDA and ALBERT who, like some unholy trinity, lighten up the darkest corners of the process of stroke recovery with some wickedly black humour.

The two characters of LIZ and SARAH serve as foils to the personalities of the stroke sufferers. Both women have good natured patience tempered with, particularly in LIZ's case, some acidic comedy observations.

There is an opportunity for doubling up on some of the smaller parts for men, for example: BOB and the VOICE OF THE BINGO CALLER; POLICEMAN and the DOCTOR.

It is important that the pace is kept up – particularly if this play is entered into a One Act Festival – as several minor set changes are needed and a slow pace by the actors could cause the play to run over the allotted time.

SCENERY
You will see from the SET PLANS at the back of the script that we have devised a set that can be very quickly transformed, which is a vital time-saver. It is also recommended that certain items are put on casters, such as BILLY's computer station; the hospital TV (which could be on a wheeled stand). Even the patient's hospital chairs could be wheelchairs if necessary.

MUSIC AND SOUND EFFECTS
The use of music is recommended when the set goes dark between scenes. However, as there are several scene breaks, we suggest that you do not use the same piece of music over and over again, as this is guaranteed to drive an adjudicator and audience up the wall!

There is much use of voices off in this play. We recommend that most of them are microphoned offstage, as this avoids the problem of actors onstage missing lines or talking over a recorded offstage voice and ruining the timing. The only exception to this is during the final scene change where BILLY is hearing voices in his nightmare. These voices could be recorded with the music and played as an all-in-one sound effect.

Other sound effects are a ringing telephone, ambulance/police sirens, banging on a door, vehicles stopping and doors slamming and a battering ram being used. All these sound effects can be sourced on the internet. Try www.sound-effects-library.com.

A STROKE OF LUCK

CAST *(In order of appearance)*

LIZ	Long suffering but good humoured woman in her late 30s – early 40s.
BILLY	Impatient and highly strung man in his early 50s.
BOB	Billy's 'Inner Angel' who appears during the stroke.
VOICE OF EMERGENCY SERVICES (999)	(woman, offstage microphone)
VOICE OF PARAMEDIC	(male, offstage)
POLICEMAN	Male, any age suitable for a serving police officer.
SARAH	An experienced and warm-hearted nurse
HILDA	Aged 70+ female patient, given to saucy comments.
SANDRA	Aged 60+ female patient, tending to be the voice of reason.
ALBERT	Aged 70+ male patient, cantankerous but funny.
VOICE OF BINGO CALLER	(male, offstage microphone)
DOCTOR	Male, any age, rather relieved to be indulging in jokey banter with a patient.
VARIOUS VOICES OFFSTAGE	(male and female)

4 male parts (with doubling) and 4 female parts. Several offstage voices which could be done by 1 man and 1 woman (SEE PRODUCER'S NOTES).

The action takes place in a kitchen and in a hospital day room.

A STROKE OF LUCK

BILLY and LIZ's kitchen. In darkness. On the worktop is an electric kettle and two mugs; a caddy for tea bags; a box of green tea bags; a bowl of sugar; several spoons; an electric toaster and a couple of plates. A fridge is presumed to be in one of the cupboards below. There are no top cupboards but there could be a 'window' with the curtains closed. On the end of the worktop there are two 'PG Tips monkeys' (large soft toys) seated together. They are 'the girls'. There is also a cordless phone on the worktop. In front of BILLY, on the kitchen table, there is a paper with instructions on, a letter and his mobile phone. By the side of the kitchen table is an overnight bag with various things in it. Downstage right is a small table with a laptop computer on it and an ashtray. Next to it is an office-type chair. BILLY is sitting at the kitchen table in his dressing gown. He is agitated. LIZ appears in the doorway, in her dressing gown. Still in the dark.

LIZ	Billy! What the hell?
BILLY	Sorry. Did I wake you?
LIZ	*(switching the kitchen light on)* I've been awake since four seventeen precisely.
BILLY	I'm sorry. I did try and sneak
LIZ	Well, next time, please try and be just a little sneakier!
BILLY	Tippy toes it is then.
LIZ	You'd never make a burglar. Anyway it wasn't your tippy-dippy-tip-toes that woke me. Why did you have to pull the chain?
BILLY	It was a number two!
LIZ	*(coming in to the kitchen and going over to the electric kettle)* Too much information thank you. Next time can you 'tippy toes' off into the woods and do it quietly. *(She switches the kettle on.)*

BILLY	It's frosty outside. You wouldn't think it could be at this time of year would you?
LIZ	Believe me, it's frosty in here right now!
BILLY	*(loudly)* I'm sorry.... all right! It's my nerves.
LIZ	No need to shout. And I could hear every single nerve too. God designed wind as a feature of the weather, not a concerto to be played on the landing. Believe you me. It's not attractive.
BILLY	Sorry.
LIZ	Anyway, what have you got to be nervous about? *(She sits down on the vacant chair at the kitchen table.)*
BILLY	Have you forgotten what day it is? And what time it is?
LIZ	*(sarcastically)* It's my day off ...a rare day off...and it's now precisely...five am. Plus the time it took to walk down the stairs...and do you know how I know that? Because I looked at my brand new digital alarm clock, which I have never heard go *off* yet, because we are always awake before *it* is.
BILLY	And you know what date it is don't you?
LIZ	Not offhand.
BILLY	It's exactly twelve months to the day. You've forgotten haven't you?
LIZ	*(realising)* Oh I see. Oh no. So that's what this is all about is it? Now you are being ridiculous.
BILLY	That's what you think but I'm taking no chances. I going to have a brew and get ready. Do you want one?
LIZ:	Seeing as I've just switched the kettle on, I may as well.

(She goes back to the worktop and starts to make two mugs of tea. Green for her, black for him.)

This is not normal behaviour. Trust me, it's not right.

BILLY   I've packed most things but I can't find any handkerchiefs. Can you have a look for me?

LIZ   *(annoyed)* Please!

BILLY   Please. I'm going to go in my thin dressing gown. No, they would only have to take the gown off again when they put me to bed. It'll save them a job. *(Takes gown off)*

(LIZ brings the mugs of tea to the table and sits. BILLY holds up a piece of A4 paper with big capital letters in one hand, and his mobile phone in the other.)

Now here's my mobile with the number on last redial for 999. The front door is unlocked and my bag is here ready. Here's what you say when you ring. *(BILLY gives LIZ the piece of paper and phone)*

LIZ   What's with all the big capital letters? Do you think I can't read? *(she reads aloud)* Say this first. 'Ambulance. Urgent. Stroke. FAST. Then say-Our postcode is CW8 1QQ. Then give full address. It speeds things up.'*(she derides him)* Do you think I can't even call an ambulance? Billy, this is absolute madness. You need to be in hospital, that's for certain! A mental hospital!

BILLY   You won't say that if I die will you?... Or worse. *If* it happens again, it's a fact, one recovers, one dies, one survives ...it's a one in three chance. I could end up as a vegetable.

LIZ   *(exasperated)* Nothing is going to happen.

BILLY	You saw them didn't you... last time? Some of the poor buggers couldn't even wipe their own arses.
LIZ	Don't say arse. It's not nice and I don't like it.
BILLY	And they'd been like that for yonks. And you know why that was, don't you? Not quick enough. It's brain damage.
LIZ	Oh it's brain damage all right!
BILLY	You've seen what it says on the TV ads haven't you? The more time you save, the more of a man you save. They said last time that if I make it through twelve months then I could stop worrying about having another stroke. And today's the day. At precisely six o'clock it will be twelve months to the minute.
LIZ:	They also said that you should get plenty of rest and sleep. You!? Need more sleep!? Hah! You're the master. You're always tired. And don't I know it!
BILLY	I could be at death's door as we speak.
LIZ	Well before you slip out of this world and in to the next, can you drink your tea? ... Though how you can drink that stuff that looks like tar and is loaded with sugar, I don't know. At least mine is healthy tea.
BILLY	Liz. Liz. Look. Tea is black. It's meant to be black. There is a white tea, I'll give you that, but it's very rare. Probably the white man messing about with it when we had an empire. But no I'm sorry green tea is not what you should be drinking, especially after what it did to me.
LIZ	Poppy cock! It was the cigarettes and alcohol more like. I'll tell you what! Never mind! You sit there and contemplate and I'll go and get changed. So if you can hang on to life, as

we know it until I get back, I'd be grateful. I don't want a dead man ruining my day off. *(looks at her watch and asks him to concur)* How many minutes...do you make it... *(sarcastic)* to lift off?

BILLY   Eighteen now.

LIZ   Well in that case I'll have time to have another cup and make you some toast. We can't have you riding in an ambulance, or a coffin, with an empty stomach now can we? Or worse still, on a vegetable barrow.

BILLY   *(hands her a letter)* Here, keep this just in case.

LIZ   In case of what?

BILLY   In case....you know.

     (LIZ exits. BILLY makes a big thing of getting his overnight bag up and going through a checklist that is in the bag.)

BILLY   Right...pyjamas...on...dressing gown...off. *(He gets a toiletries bag out of the overnight bag and checks its contents)* deodorant...razor...gel...aftershave...comb... tablets...they'll have gas and air there. *(He puts the toiletries bag back and checks other items)* Slippers...book...not that I'll be able to read it but you never know...personal information about next of kin etcetera, etcetera.

     (BILLY puts the bag at the side of the table again, looks at his watch and sits, staring forward, waiting and then he rests his head on his arms on the table and falls asleep. LIZ re-enters, in her daytime clothes. She is still carrying the letter. She sees BILLY is asleep but double checks that he has a pulse. He murmurs a bit and shifts position but stays asleep. LIZ sits down with a sigh.)

LIZ   Some day off this is. At least one of us is getting some sleep. *(She mocks BILLY while he sleeps. She mimics him sarcastically)* 'I can't do it'...' I've had a stroke you know'... 'I can't go'... 'I've had a stroke you know'. 'I'm the only one in the world who's ever had a stroke'. I've never known anybody milk it more than you do Billy. I wish you'd make more of an effort in other departments as you do getting out of things. All I do is dream of having a child of our own. *(Jabbing her finger at the sleeping BILLY.)* My biological clock is ticking.... You could write a book on ways to avoid getting a girl pregnant, and remember I'm still a girl compared to you aren't I? *(LIZ takes out the letter from her pocket.)*

(she sighs) I don't know... what woman in her right mind wants a baby a fortnight before the menopause? *(Toys with letter and reads envelope)* 'To be opened in the event of my death or worse still if I become a vegetable'. *(She giggles and strokes his face tenderly)* Couch potato, definitely. *(She opens letter)* I shouldn't. *(She reads)*

'My Dearest Liz'...Huh! I'm his dearest now am I? Trust me Billy, I'm not at all dear. I'm very cheap to keep if you ask me.

'By the time you read this I could be in heaven'...Not a chance in a million. 'Or worse still, stroke hell'.....Oh! The drama of it!

'I just wanted you to know that you have been the best thing to ever happen to me in my life'...*(forgivingly)* You silly old drama queen...

'I have never ever loved anybody as much in my life as I have you'...*(disappointed)* Oh, now he's overdoing it!

'I know that sometimes I might have been difficult to live with'...No my little Spud U Like, you were bloody impossible.

Listen to me! 'I'm' making it sound as though he's actually gone. You are impossible. *(She checks BILLY's pulse again, just to make sure.)*

No you're not gone, are you my very own King Edward?

'We know that life is too short to waste and needs to be lived to the full, so please don't sit around moping. I want you to go out and enjoy the time you have left' ...that's kind of you. 'If you meet someone else and find some sort of happiness that could last forever please do not worry that you are betraying me because you are not and don't think about me when you are doing it with somebody else' .... Oh!.....That's terrible...*(milk the joke here)*. He's left out all the punctuation!

'Please remember these words' ...believe me, Billy, I'll have a job forgetting them.

P.S. Look after the girls won't you?

You silly bugger!

(She goes up to the worktop and pours some more water in her cup. She touches the monkeys.) Don't worry girls, he's not going anywhere. *(Looks at BILLY)* I don't know about you, Mister, but I'm ready for another cup. *(She picks up the overnight bag)* And I don't think you'll be needing this.

(LIZ kisses BILLY on top of his head then exits, clutching the letter, the overnight bag and her cup of tea, and we see him sleeping but very restless. Lights go down. LIZ appears

downstage in a spotlight talking on her mobile phone.)

LIZ   But I have to be firm with him otherwise....well you know what he's like...love is not always a many splendid thing, sometimes it's bloody impossible. But then I remember, I thought I might have lost him. *(listens)* Yes. He would. He'd find his way back to haunt me. *(listens)* It was. *(listens)* No he's asleep at the moment. *(listens)* He laughs about it now but then when I think back, Oh my God. *(listens)* It was exactly twelve months ago today.

(MUSIC. LIGHTS fade to black.)

(When the lights come up again, BILLY is dressed in casual clothes (could be jeans and tee shirt) and seated at his laptop typing. He gets up and goes over to the cupboard and the fridge and begins to gather things needed for a brew...cup, sugar and spoon. He is talking to himself.)

BILLY   Damn! No milk.....and no tea! Too bloody busy to get any shopping in. Billy... you need to get a grip of the situation. *(He finds a jar in the cupboard)* Coffee whitener. This'll do. I'll have a coffee for a change. *(Looks in the cupboards)* Oh no, there's whitener but no bloody coffee. This is no way to run an empire. *(Finds a strange packet and reads the label)* Green tea? Green tea? How come she remembers to get this stuff but not normal tea? *(Strokes the monkeys' heads and talks to them)* What say you girls? If it weren't for me, you'd still be a prisoner in a box, deep in Co-op Country. There's absolutely no point in working from home if you haven't got your home comforts. I'd be better off going into the office. *(He switches the kettle on)* Anyway it's LADIES day in the office and we all know what day that is, don't we girls? You don't? Well let me tell you. L.A.D.I.E.S stands for Leave And

Don't Inform Anyone Senior. Yes, I know anyone begins with A and not E but it sounds the same doesn't it? And anyway, it's never written down. Well who would? It's like POETS day. Piss Off Early Tomorrow's Saturday.

Oh bugger it. *(Takes green tea, puts a bag in the cup and pours on the water)*. It's not PG Tips. Girls, look the other way. *(BILLY makes a brew. He looks in the cup disgustedly and takes a drink)* And this is supposed to be healthy? Shuukkkk! I want to throw up. I need something to take the taste away. Where are my ciggies? *(BILLY sits back at the computer and starts typing, while dragging at a cigarette. He puts the cigarette from his left hand into the ashtray, but his hand trembles and then he can't move it properly. He makes several attempts to pick up the cigarette but he can't get his hand to work properly. This is where the stroke begins.)*

BILLY   Jesus wept. Green tea eh? Maybe I've been wrong about it. No wonder she's been supping this stuff. Feel stoned. Need water. Crack of dawn and it's as though I'm on crack. As if I knew what crack was really like.

(BILLY tries to stand up and walk back to the sink. His legs start to weaken and he slumps slowly to the floor in front of the kitchen table. BOB enters and looks concerned. He has a ghost like white face and is dressed exactly like BILLY. It appears that his job is to be motivational. When BILLY tries to speak we hear him begin to slur slightly. His tongue starts to fall out of his mouth. His slur gradually becomes worse.)

BILLY   I need a bloody doctor, I do. Where's the phone gone?

BOB   Where it always is. Come on look up.

BILLY   Who's that?

BOB	I'm you. Your spirit if you want to be precise...it's not that simple....look at me. I'm you.
BILLY	But you're up there. An angel? Ugly for an angel.
BOB	They're much further up. And I'm making sure you don't get past me to meet them. I'm more what they call in the trade 'An Out Of Body Experience' which is not the same as The Jimmy Hendrix experience.
BILLY	You're a bloody comedian.
BOB	No you are. You're thinking the thoughts and I'm telling you what they are.
BILLY	Liz does that.
BOB	I'm the part of you that stops you walking in front of a car when you are so pissed you don't know what day it is. If I had a job title I suppose I would be your 'Shutzengel'... 'Guardian angel'... 'Inner Angel'. Yes I like that. So! No heaven for you today. You're a fighter aren't you!? Now turn your head to the phone.
BILLY	I can't. I can't lift my head. I think I'm dying.
BOB	Fight it. Come on bloody well fight it.
BILLY	I can't move my leg...my arm. (BILLY can't do anything now with his left arm or leg) Who the hell are you, anyway really?
BOB	I told you. You! And I'm going to get 'us' out of here. Get a grip!
BILLY	Giiiirrrrrrlllllls help.
BOB	You will die if you rely on two stuffed monkeys to get you out of this.

(BILLY can only breathe the words out. He cannot form his

words. He slurs.)

BILLY   Lizzzzzzzzz..... I'm dying

BOB   Don't be stupid. Liz can't hear you. She's away at her
sister's. Remember? No! Jesus is your man. He'll save you. If
he's up yet. Shout him.

BILLY   *(whispers, rather weakly)* Jesuuussssssssssssssss.

BOB   Too quiet! Take deep breaths and get some steam up.

    *(BILLY starts to make himself breath very loudly hoping he
will be heard.)*

BOB   That's the spirit. Breathe really loudly.

BILLY   *(Tries to shout but it's still weak)*
Jessssssssuuuuuuuuuuuuuussssssssssssssssssss

BOB   A little better. Not coming, is he? Must be thinking of
sending the Grim Reaper instead. *(BILLY tries to move his
body while BOB reflects)*

BILLY   *(squirming on the ground in distress)* I'm dying!

BOB   No you're not! Not today. You haven't said goodbye to Liz.
Come on make an effort.

BILLY   Jessuuuusssssssss.....Hellllllllllllllllllllllllllp
Jessssuuuuuuuuuus.

BOB   Better but still no sign. He's probably healing the sick
somewhere or maybe he's tending his flock. Perhaps it's
national flock week in Wales or something. Let's try plan B.

BILLY   Which is?

BOB   The NHS. Some say it's quite good if you're really poorly.
And you look at death's door. No offence intended.

BILLY   None taken.

BOB	Try 999.
BILLY	Phone! Phone! Phone! ET phone home.
BOB	This is no time for jokes. Come on get a grip.
	(BILLY pushes himself along the floor to the worktop where the cordless phone is. Slowly and laboriously, gasping for breath. He makes it to the phone and manages to drag it next to him on the floor. He can only use his right side for everything. He dials 999).
BOB	Be careful! You've got the phone upside down! You'll get 666, and then you're really in it. *(He laughs)*
999	*(Phone is answered. Voice offstage.)* 999 Emergency. Which service do you require?
BILLY	*(He manages to make these words understood)* Can you smell burning?
999	No sir.
BILLY	Well you had better just send a bloody ambulance. And don't ask Jesus to drive. He's too busy tending. I'm dying.
BOB	This is no time for being flippant, you moron! Just get on with it!
999	Hello. Hello. Is this some kind of a hoax call? It's a serious offence you know!
BILLY	No! No! No! Helllllp. I'm Dying!!!!!
999	Ok sir. I hear you properly now. Ambulance. What is your address? What is your postcode?
	(This is where BILLY'S speech becomes really bad and into a full slur, alternating with some good speech. He can say some things but he cannot say 'sixteen'.For some reason, he

can say fifteen and seventeen.)

999	*(repeats)* What is your postcode?
BILLY	Theee wwwwwwwwwway on... cue cue
BOB	Come on brain, help the mouth.
999	Sir was that CW8 1QQ?
BILLY	Yetttthhhhh.
BOB	Well done so far.
999	House number?
BILLY	Thhhhhixxxxxxteeeeeeeeee
999	Was that number sixty sir?
BOB	She can't understand you.
999	Have you been drinking sir?
BOB	Come on mouth.
BILLY	Nooo ... thhhhhixxxxxxteeeeeeeeee...
999	Sorry sir, I didn't get that ...
BILLY	It's before seventeen.
999	Is that four, seventeen...four one seven Sir? Is that correct?
BILLY	No! Before seventeen...after fifteen
999	Is that fifteen sir? One five?
BILLY	No! After fifteen
BOB	Come on or we'll be here all day or worse. Make an effort. Shout!
BILLY	*(giving a desperate yell)* Thixteen!
BOB	Better.
999	Sixteen sir? Is that it?

BILLY	Yeth. Yeth.
999	Ambulance on its way to you sir. It won't be long. A suspected stroke by the sound of you.
BILLY	Stroke my arse. It's that green tea. It's drugs.
999	Did you say something sir?
BILLY	I'm dying.
999	Don't worry sir. We don't let anybody die on our shift. Too much paperwork.
BOB	She'll be thinking, there's always one isn't there? One funny bugger. She can give it too. *(There is the sound of an ambulance siren, getting louder, and then the scrunch of a vehicle stopping. BILLY shouts, slurred.)*
BILLY:	Jesssuuuuuuus! Help!...In here!...In here!...In here!
	(Sounds of a commotion outside. There is banging on the front door)
PARAMEDIC	*(offstage)* Are you able to open the door, sir?
BILLY	*(As loud as he can)* Nooo.
PARAMEDIC	*(offstage)* The door won't open sir.
	(There is the sound of another siren, getting louder and vehicle stopping)
BILLY	*(gains all his strength, draws all his breath and shouts.)* Kick the bloody door in. I'll pay for it. *(BILLY slumps as if unconscious and his breathing becomes shallow.)*
PARAMEDIC	*(offstage)* It's all right, sir. The police have arrived and they are going to break the door down!
	(There is a sound of a battering ram being applied to the door. Then a POLICEMAN enters with a battering ram,

puts it down and kneels beside BILLY)

POLICEMAN   I've had to break in twice this week to get the crew in.

(BILLY looks up and with all his strength raises his right arm and cries out)

BILLY   Ahhh! Jesus has come at last...and he's come as a bloody

policeman! *(BILLY passes out)*

(MUSIC. LIGHTS fade quickly to black. MUSIC continues until LIGHTS fade up. The scene is a hospital lounge. There are chairs in a semi-circle, with pull-over tables in front of them. BILLY is in the far stage left chair with a drip feed by the side of him. Billy's legs should be raised on something to make it appear to be a lounger chair and a blanket should cover him. He needs to be leaning back on cushions. Seated in the other chairs are HILDA, SANDRA and ALBERT. The nurse, SARAH, is fiddling with BILLY's drip feed. There is a television on a low table at the side of the stage and a plastic chair at the back centre stage.) (see PRODUCER'S NOTES and SET PLAN)

HILDA   Look at him the poor devil. He's out of it. Why on earth have they got him out of bed and in to a chair so soon? It's madness.

SARAH   Never mind all that. It comes from the top. It's the new way. We've got to encourage patients to become mobile. We just do what we're told. Besides, we're so short staffed and we can't be in two places at once.

SANDRA   So you're getting *us* to look after him. Is that it?

SARAH   No of course not. It's called fast tracking. Fast mobility.

ALBERT   She's making it up as she goes along.

SARAH	Maybe if we'd started it when *you* came in, you might be further on by now.
HILDA	I can't see me getting any better.
SANDRA	Me neither.
ALBERT	No work for me today again that's for sure, although I've been worse.
HILDA	He doesn't look right. It's as if he's not with us....not all there.... don't you think?
SANDRA	Did we all look as bad as that when we came in? I can't remember.
ALBERT	If anyone's not all there, you should look closer to home, Hilda.
HILDA	That's no way to talk to me. You always want to make me appear to be a halfwit or something.
ALBERT	Yes perhaps you're right. I'm sorry. You're definitely not a halfwit. You'd have to be a little cleverer to be one of those.
HILDA	Are you going to just stand there and let him speak to me like that Sarah?
SARAH	What can I do?
HILDA	You're in charge aren't you?
SARAH	Oh, all right. Albert! Please don't upset the other patients!
ALBERT	Yah voll..... Mein Fuhrer.
SANDRA	How old do you think he is? He's not a bad looking man is he Sarah? He doesn't look like the stroke type, does he?
SARAH	A bit too old for me, but I can see how he might appeal to you. That's the thing now. They do seem to be happening younger. We've got one or two in their thirties in the other

	ward. And a bit...well.......you know...fit. Now, they will be getting double bed baths.
HILDA	Ooh! I'll help you love!
ALBERT	*(tutting)* As long as it's in trousers. You'd think she'd never seen a bloke before! There are rules about that sort of thing in her majesty's detention centre. *(To BILLY)* Prison... that's what it is in here mate. And *she (Looks at SARAH)* is one of the main guards. You won't get out alive.
SARAH	And what's this about a prison? We don't keep you here. In fact you are quite lucky to be here if you ask me. If anyone can get you back to normal...I use the word loosely...we can. Maybe if you'd been left much longer before you came in it might be a little different. You might never recover... fully...but we'll have you back in the community, don't you worry Albert. Then they can share in the pleasure you give us.
	I know you don't believe it at the moment, but believe you me, getting in here, as quickly as possible has been a stroke of luck, especially for him. *(points to BILLY)* We have a better chance of helping a speedy recovery.
ALBERT	So we're lucky are we? We're in a sort of prison at the mercy of the commandant. Half of us can't wipe our own arses. And the food is like prison food.
SANDRA	Rubbish.
ALBERT	Have you ever been inside one then?
SANDRA	Of course I haven't. Don't be silly.
ALBERT	So how do you know it's not like prison?
HILDA	That's just stupid talk. Have *you* ever been inside a prison?
ALBERT	Well I was in a prisoner of war camp once.

SANDRA	*(sounding sympathetic)* Pay no attention to her. Oh, I'm sorry Albert. We didn't realise. Were you really a POW, Albert? How long for? All through the war?
ALBERT	No just for a month. In the middle of summer it was.
SANDRA	What was it like?
ALBERT	Well it chucked it down for the first two weeks but it picked up slightly at the end. We won't be booking again that's for sure. All those bloody Germans. We couldn't get a sun bed near the pool for love nor money. Oh no! It's Britain for us from now on.
	(The two women realise they've been duped and tut loudly. They all look at BILLY)
BILLY	Nnnnnnnnnnnnnn
	(LIZ arrives with shopping bag)
LIZ	Just look at you Billy! He's not even recognised me. What are you doing out of bed? Nurse…should he be? Where can I find a doctor? I want a word with him. He doesn't look comfortable to me.
SARAH	We try to begin rehabilitation as soon as we can. It gives more of a chance according to the experts.
LIZ	But this seems little premature even to my inexperienced eye. Where can I find a chair?
SARAH	I'll see if I can find you one… *(SARAH exits)*
ALBERT	*(to LIZ)* There's a chair over there by the curtain, but as for finding a doctor…it would be easier to knit fog.
HILDA	It always looks bad at first love. We all come in like that. Pay no attention to him. He'll be much better soon. You just

wait and see.

LIZ   Thanks. It is worry isn't it? I've never seen him as bad as this. Mind you he has come home in some states. Usually he has a glazed look about him but his look is more like a haunted look as if he's seen a ghost. *(LIZ goes and gets the chair and sets it down by BILLY)* I was at my sister's and no one knew how to get hold of me.

HILDA   Like a spirit you mean? My husband had that look about him.

LIZ   From a stroke?

HILDA   Oh no! When we buried him.

SANDRA   That's a terrible thing to say.

LIZ   No! Not so much like a spirit. More *full* of spirits. I tried to tell him. What....with the drink... and the cigarettes....it was either this or a heart attack. Mind you, they do say a heart attack is better.

ALBERT   As long as you live through it. *(indicating BILLY)* So he likes a couple then? There's nothing wrong with that.

LIZ   Oh! He's had a couple before the pub door closes behind us.

HILDA   My hubby was like that. Pisces you know. *(reflects)* Maybe that's why he drank like a fish.

LIZ   Yes, I see what you mean. My Billy's a Pisces too. Must be something in it, I suppose.

SANDRA   Well there's no bar in here, sweetheart, so he's safe from that, for the time being. Albert has it sneaked in you know.

LIZ   Oh, he'll be getting no booze from me. That's for sure. Not for a long... long time.

BILLY   Lllllllliiii…

LIZ	Oh, sorry! I've not even spoken to you yet have I sweet? Billy… Billy… How are you angel? You look like death warmed up. *(She fusses over him. Takes a comb out of her bag and combs his hair.)*
ALBERT	*(to the others)* He must have something, the lad. His girlfriend, if that's who she is…and I think she must be… wasn't smacked with the ugly stick. And younger than him is my guess.
SANDRA	She could be his wife for all we know. Not his daughter that's for sure. Anyway it's none of our business.
ALBERT	No she's not his wife. I'm certain of that.
HILDA	She seems to be very close to him whoever she is.
SANDRA	Albert will figure it out. He'll know who she is before long. Albert knows everything
ALBERT	Didn't you notice in the ward, over his bed? Am I the only one?
HILDA	Noticed! Noticed what?
ALBERT	His name.
SANDRA	What's wrong with Billy? It's a nice name. After all, it's short for William.
HILDA	Yes, and there have been lots of famous Williams haven't there? Like…William Shakespeare…William of Orange…William Wordsworth…William Pitt the Younger.
ALBERT	What is this? A general knowledge quiz?
HILDA	William Pitt the Elder…
SANDRA	William the Conqueror…
ALBERT	For goodness sake!
HILDA	William Pitt…

SANDRA	You said him already.
HILDA	William Tell…and William Clinton…I did not have sexual relations…
SANDRA	Trust you to think of him! We used to grow William pears you know…
ALBERT	How long is this going to go on for?
SANDRA	Then there's Willy Rushton and Willy Russell
HILDA	And of course 'Free Willy'. That's the best kind, don't you think? It should be on the national health. Free at the point of use.
ALBERT	Very clever, aren't we all? But, I was in fact, referring to his surname. It's Nomates. As in Billy Nomates. As in…. 'On your own'…
LIZ	*(overhearing this last bit)* Actually, it's pronounced 'Nomatees'
BILLY	nnnnnnnnnnnnnnnnnnnnnnnn
HILDA	*(giggling)* That's good, 'cos you wouldn't want to be Mrs Nomates…would you?
LIZ	*(getting a little annoyed)* I'm sorry?
SANDRA	Oh take no notice of her, dear. She's senile, as well as having had a stroke. Are you his wife love?
LIZ	Oh no, not yet.
SANDRA	Well I'm Sandra, this is Hilda. And 'that over there' is Albert.
LIZ	I'm Liz.
HILDA	Well he's at your mercy now darling. Get a ring on his finger. We'll be witnesses. *(laughs)*
ALBERT	But he can't say 'I do', can he? So it seems like a pointless

exercise.

SANDRA   *(laughing)* Make him sign an X . Hold his hand and move the pen.

LIZ   *(laughing as well)* One day maybe but not today. Where's that nurse gone?

ALBERT   She's busy..... pretending to be busy. They're all very good at that in here.

LIZ   But how is he going to manage? He can't be left on his own in this state.

HILDA   Don't you fret love, we'll keep an eye on him and if need be we'll shout. That nurse, Sarah, is not as bad as the rest. She does come when she's called.

SANDRA   We manage. We have to. Just so long as we have no real emergencies such as Albert running out of Guinness.

HILDA   Yes, these nurses are a bit rough and ready, but they do their best, and they don't shout rape, when Albert feels their backsides. He does it all the time.

LIZ   Don't you go putting ideas in his head! *(To BILLY)* Never mind nurses' bums Billy. You keep your hands to yourself. Do you hear?

BILLY   Aarrrrsse

LIZ   Billy! See he can still say arse. Amazing isn't it? He gets to death's door and when I visit, does he want to tell me he loves me? Does he want to whisper sweet nothings in my ear? No he wants to swear and say arse. Well I swear one thing Billy boy, you had better get on that road to recovery and fast. *(whispering to Billy)* I want a little Billy. My body clock is running. Don't think you can use having a stroke as an excuse. You won't get away with it even if I have to get the doctors to join us together. I want impregnating. *(raises voice)* I want a baby!

HILDA   Ooh, I say!

(BILLY manages to raise his right arm slightly and LIZ cuddles up to him)

BILLY   Liiiiii…

ALBERT   Well, you've got a baby now…whether you like it or not! *(points at BILLY)* He'll need a nappy, poor sod.

LIZ   *(half laughing)* He did wear one once…. a nappy I mean…. in the village pram race. He looked cute I thought. Not very baby like though. He had his stubbly beard. Not quite the same is it? I don't want my baby to have stubble.

HILDA   Oh no dear. It's definitely no good on a baby. You'd get chapped legs giving birth to a baby with stubble.

(SARAH brings in the meals, on a trolley, under covered plates.)

SARAH   I couldn't find a spare chair…oh, you've got one…that's good. Right, time for grub! And it's uncanny. You've all ordered the same again.

ALBERT   Another lesson from Masterchef. Now that the smoked salmon and cream cheese is off the menu we're having the gruel- a- l-etouffee, again.

SARAH   Yes, but it's low cholesterol gruel. *(She dispenses the plates on to everyone's tables, except for BILLY)* It's good for you, so eat up.

LIZ   Is it ok if I stay and help Billy?

SARAH	You can stay of course you can.
ALBERT	Watch it, girl! She'll have you doing the washing up!
SARAH	But I'm sorry, at the moment Billy is nil by mouth.
LIZ	Nil by mouth? What does that mean?
ALBERT	It means, love, that he's not allowed anything in his mouth, including gruel, drink, or dummies. You're not allowed anything to pass your lips. Not until you can swallow properly.
LIZ	So how does he get his food? Is it all by a drip?
ALBERT	Oh no. They stick it up your jacksy. Then you clench your bum cheeks and roll round the bed. Well it does need to be well chewed, you know.
BILLY	Aaarse.
	(HILDA cackles)
SARAH	Albert! That's quite enough. Any more of that and I will have to report you. *(SARAH begins to help to sit Billy up)*
ALBERT	You cheeky monkey.
LIZ	And that reminds me Billy, I've brought the girls to see you.
SANDRA	That's nice. So he has daughters from a previous.....
	(LIZ pulls out the two monkeys from her bag)
LIZ	These are the girls.
ALBERT	*(aside)* They're ugly babies.
SANDRA	They're toys.
ALBERT	I know that.
	(SARAH moves to lift BILLY out of the chair and adjust his position)

LIZ	Oh, here let me help you ...
SARAH	No don't worry, it's ok. We're trained for this. We get special instructions in how to pick men up.
HILDA	Sounds like my kind of job!
SARAH	There we are Billy. That must feel better.
LIZ	Yes Billy, you look so much better sat up like that. I'll go and see if I can find the doctor. *(patting the monkeys)* Keep an eye on him won't you girls?

(MUSIC. LIGHTS fade to black)

(MUSIC continues until the LIGHTS come up again. The plates, the monkeys and the trolley have disappeared. The tables are pushed to one side of each chair. HILDA, SANDRA, ALBERT and BILLY are all watching TV. They all have trouble keeping their left arms on their knees and are all constantly pulling their arms back in to place. The TV is crackling. SANDRA is looking at the TV guide. BILLY is somewhat improved. His speech is slightly slurred but he has obviously made great improvements.)

HILDA	What's the matter with the telly now? It was ok last night.
ALBERT	It's those nurses. They spend all night watching movies when we are all tucked up. I know they do, and they're supposed to be working.No sooner are we strapped in, and they're off. It's beer and sandwiches and feet up. I've even smelled curry on a couple of occasions.
HILDA	No wonder no one ever comes when I'm dying to pee. My bladder muscles have never worked so hard.
ALBERT	Why don't you use one of those cardboard buckets?
SANDRA	Oh it's ok for you. In case you hadn't noticed, we are built

differently.

ALBERT   It wouldn't do if we were all built the same would it? Well there would be no need for the maternity ward for a start. More nappies for us.

BILLY   Oh don't mention maternity wards and nappies for goodness sake.

SANDRA   Oh yes your Liz is hoping isn't she?

BILLY   Well she can hope for a little longer. I'm out of action at the moment.

ALBERT   They did that to us in the war you know.

BILLY   Did what?

ALBERT   Put us out of commission for a while. Something in the tea. To stop us thinking about...well you know.

BILLY   It wasn't green tea by any chance was it?

ALBERT   What's that?

BILLY   Oh it doesn't matter.

SANDRA   I wish we could sort out the TV.

BILLY   Well no one else will. So it's left to James Bond here. You keep nicks then, while I sort it out.

(As no one can walk, BILLY slides off his chair on to the ground and pushes himself on his belly to the TV and rescues the remote controller. He begins his journey back to his chair, when SARAH walks in and catches him.)

SARAH   Billy! What on earth do you think you are doing?

ALBERT   Don't move Billy! She might be armed. *(ALBERT looks disapprovingly at SARAH)* He's stealing the programme changer, and then he plans to tunnel to the private wards...

...Code 3.......Code 3......Man down...... Caught trying to escape. He's armed and dangerous. Cuff him nurse. He has a TV remote and he might try to use it.

(SARAH pulls BILLY up on to his chair)

SARAH   Now don't let me catch you again Billy or I'll.....

BILLY   Keep me after class?

ALBERT   Shoot him nurse. He'll thank you one day.

SARAH   *(to ALBERT)* I'll shoot you in a minute. It's not funny. I could get a bad back and a girl in my position needs a good strong back. *(SARAH exits tutting)*

HILDA   *(whispers)* She likes doctors, you know.

ALBERT: Well you have to laugh in here. Otherwise we'd all go bonkers.

BILLY   Yes, it's just like 'One flew over the cuckoo's nest in here'

HILDA   Poor old Billy. What's up with your cuckoo then?

SANDRA   You leave his cuckoo alone. You'll be embarrassing him...
            ..and me too, by the way.

BILLY   Oh don't worry about me. I'm not bothered. We're all in the same boat here, aren't we? Knackered.

ALBERT   We've only got half of our bodies working. Nobody wants half a man.

HILDA   *(cheekily)* Depends which half, if you ask me.

ALBERT   Well no one wants half a woman either. It'd be just my luck. If I won half a woman in a raffle, I'd win the half that talks.

SANDRA   Right! That's enough! Who's got the TV Times? What's on next?

ALBERT	You've got it.
SANDRA	Oh, so I have…now let's have a look. Channel 1…Doctor in the house – A Comedy…
ALBERT	No comment.
SANDRA	Channel 2 – General Hospital.
ALBERT	She's having a laugh!
SANDRA	No I am not. I'm just reading what it says in here.
HILDA:	Here, Sandra, let me have a look.

(SANDRA passes the TV paper to HILDA)

SANDRA	I've no reason to lie, you know.
HILDA	I know, dear, but you know what he's like. Let's see… Channel 3 – Emergency ward 10…Channel 4 – Animal hospital…
ALBERT	That does it! Nurse! Give me the injection! You've beaten me.
HILDA	*(looking at ALBERT)* Well… look for yourself.
ALBERT	Yes! Give me that paper. It's bad enough being locked up here……without all the propaganda programmes. They are trying to brainwash us.

(HILDA passes paper to ALBERT. He looks at the paper)

ALBERT	*(disgusted)* Ok you win. You got me.
BILLY:	Here, Albert, let me have a look. *(BILLY takes the paper)*
BILLY:	*(BILLY starts chuckling)* You couldn't make it up. Sky 1 – Carry on Nursing, Sky 2- A hospital drama, Sky 3 – Doctor Finlay's Case Book. Oh here's one for you Albert. – 'I'm a grump get me out of here'.
ALBERT	I've seen that.

HILDA	Don't be daft, he just made it up.
ALBERT	I have. I have seen it before. It starred Tom Hanks.
SANDRA	That's Forest Gump, you silly old sod. Run Forest! Run!
BILLY	Here! This looks good. It looks like a thriller. It's called 'The Plumington Patient Poisoner'
MUSIC	*(EVERYONE laughs. MUSIC. LIGHTS fade to black. continues until LIGHTS come up. The setting is the same but everyone has gone except SARAH and BILLY. They are sitting in two of the chairs with a table between them. SARAH is making BILLY follow certain exercises with his left hand on the table. Touching finger and thumb together and then repeat with each finger)*
SARAH	That's good, Billy. Much better. Now take your forefinger, like this. Try to copy what I am doing. Now starting with your forefinger, make each finger touch your thumb. *(BILLY makes his left hand watch his right hand and copy. He is in distress about his fingers not moving.)*
BILLY	It's no good. My fingers won't move. I'm getting brain ache. For Christ sake fingers.....move! Left hand, just copy right hand will you? It's no good. I'm tired.
SARAH	It's normal. We'll get you there. Now push against my hand. *(They push left hands together)* That's much better. You're doing great. We just need to be sure that you have the ability to do basic things, before the consultant will sign you out.
BILLY	Liz keeps saying she wants me to do basic things too.
SARAH	Not those sort of things, Billy. That's a different matter altogether. We can give you pills for that, but we can't give you pills that can cook your dinner and wash the pots... or

	wash yourself. That's what matters now.
BILLY	Well can't you give me home visits for bath time then?
SARAH	Don't be smutty Billy. We have pills than can control smuttiness too.
BILLY	I'm joking. It seems as though there are pills for everything except stubborn fingers.
SARAH	Silly me. I forgot to give you one of those. They're this big *(demonstrates massive)* and they are suppositories.
BILLY	Ouch.
SARAH	*(they put their palms together and push hard. BILLY gives way)* Now let's see how you are with your walking.
	(BILLY stands and begins to walk up and down the ward, limping badly but supporting himself.)
SARAH	Wow! I am impressed. You could be playing like Beckham soon.
BILLY	That's good because I couldn't even kick a ball before.
SARAH	The consultant will be pleased with you. I wouldn't be surprised if he doesn't give you the all clear. How does that feel?
BILLY	You just give me the hoops and I'll jump through them. What's next?
SARAH	It's the hard part. I'm afraid. The stairs. We need you to do the stairs again to show you can get up and down. And then the kitchen to show you can hold a pan and boil a kettle. You need to be able to use one hand at least.
BILLY	You lead the way then…and be prepared to be amazed….
	(SARAH and BILLY exit. MUSIC. LIGHTS fade to black.

MUSIC continues until the LIGHTS come up again, to show a fed-up BILLY sitting in his chair, with SARAH standing over him. HILDA, SANDRA and ALBERT are all seated in their chairs.)

SARAH   Not to worry, Billy. You did well but a few more days will make all the difference. You will be going home but not this week. You'll see. Your speech is certainly better than what it was. I thought you said 'arse' brilliantly this morning.

BILLY   Oh yes, I'm sorry, Sarah. It just that it seemed so near but then so far. A million miles away. I'm never going to get back to where I was am I?

SARAH   Truth? Some people make a full recovery... or to be totally accurate, a 'fairly full recovery' which is a good thing. It's all about little steps along the way. Anyway, you'll be able to talk a lot more about how you feel and ask more questions tomorrow. The consultant is coming to talk to you.

(VOICE OF BINGO CALLER offstage, on a microphone)

CALLER   Is everyone ready for bingo, then?

(There are a few feeble voices calling "Yes" offstage)

ALBERT   *(scornfully)* So this is our big surprise is it?

SARAH   Yes. I know it's not for everybody but we do these things for your own good. Believe it or not, bingo can be very therapeutic.

ALBERT   How do you work that out when it's only the brain dead that play it in the first place?

SARAH   Well......you're holding pencils....you're reading numbers... and marking them as you hear them.........it's coordination. It helps you to concentrate. Here Albert, have a book just in case you decide to join in with us. Think concentration.

(SARAH gives ALBERT a book of bingo games)

ALBERT   *(to the others)* I told you. This is a 'concentration' camp.

SANDRA   Albert! Shut it! It makes a change. I'm looking forward to it.

HILDA   It's beneath you is it Albert?

ALBERT   Well just look at the sort of people that go.

SANDRA   Not at all what you are used to eh? Albert. *(To BILLY)* Albert prefers the company of celebrities. Don't you Albert?

HILDA   Oh yes. He's mixed with the upper echelons all right. Can I tell him Albert? Tell Billy who you met.

ALBERT   If you must.

HILDA   He's only been out with none other than…Vera Lynn.

BILLY   What! As in… Dame Vera Lynn?… as in the fishmongers daughter?… 'Whale meet again'?

ALBERT   You can mock.

BILLY   You'll be telling us next that you've been out with Royalty. The Queen maybe? Eh?….Albert?…Eh….Eh..?

ALBERT   Don't be daft. Of course I didn't go out with the Queen. *(pause)* My pal Eddy did. I was with Vera wasn't I? We all went together.

BILLY   So you and your mate were on a double date with Vera Lynn and the Queen…is that right??

ALBERT   Well to be truthful.

SANDRA   Oh here it comes. The truth.

ALBERT   Elizabeth was only a Princess at the time.

            (The women snort derisively.)

BILLY   Ah yes of course. And where did you take them Albert?

ALBERT	Where do you think? To the local pub of course!
HILDA	And no one recognised Vera Lynn? Not to mention the future Queen of England!
ALBERT	No! Vera sat with her back to everyone and Elizabeth was wearing casual clothes.
CALLER	Testing, testing...
SARAH	I think it's going to start. Have you all got your pens and pencils ready?
SANDRA	I've brought my lucky pencil.
ALBERT	*(To SARAH)* See what I mean?
	(ALBERT grudgingly helps himself to a pencil from SARAH)
CALLER	Five and nine!
ALBERT	Five and nine......fifty nine. That was the fifty nine bus service from London to Brighton, you know.
CALLER	Number eight!
ALBERT	*(poking HILDA)* One fat lady!
HILDA	Who are you calling fat?
ALBERT	If the cap fits...
CALLER	Five and six!
ALBERT	Was she worth it?
HILDA	Are you being rude again?
CALLER	Eight and nine!
ALBERT	Nearly there.
CALLER	Two little ducks!

ALBERT	Not our dinner. That's for sure. Quack Quack.
CALLER	Those legs eleven!
ALBERT	A very unfortunate centipede.
CALLER	All the fours!
SANDRA AND HILDA	*(they giggle)* Droopy drawers!
SARAH	How are you doing so far Billy?
BILLY	Not a single number.
SARAH	I mean, how are you coping?
BILLY	Oh fine... and I can hold the pen. Look!
SARAH	Good.
CALLER	Doctors orders!
ALBERT	Number nine.
SANDRA	I thought you never played bingo Albert?
ALBERT	I don't.
CALLER	One and six. That's sweet sixteen.
HILDA	*(grinning at ALBERT)* That's me, that is. Sweet sixteen.
ALBERT	*(looking at her in disbelief)* You couldn't be sweet sixteen after ten pints.
CALLER	Unlucky for some.
HILDA	HOUSE!
CALLER	Just a moment...I think someone on Morrison Ward called House.
HILDA	Yes. Me!
CALLER	Have you got the last number called – sixteen?

HILDA	No!
CALLER	Well it's unlucky for you isn't it?
HILDA	*(glaring up at the ceiling, thinking that's where the CALLER is)* You swine! Are you any relation to Albert?
	(MUSIC. LIGHTS fade to black. MUSIC continues until LIGHTS come up again. BILLY is sitting on his own, trying to read a book. A DOCTOR enters.)
DOC	Hello Billy. I'm new to this hospital and I am now your consultant, if that's Ok with you. Anyway let me introduce myself. I'm known..... in the trade as it were...as Doctor Bed...good.
BILLY	That's a lot to live up to. Is that as in bedside manner....or between the sheets, doctor?
DOC	We doctors never have time for our own beds. I can only get a good night's sleep when I'm sick and you could say, unfortunately for me, I never am.
BILLY	Well don't pick a stroke. Go for a heart attack. I've heard they're easier.
DOC	Both are to be avoided if possible.
BILLY	But you can get a new heart right? But no one could replace a brain like mine *(laughs)*. Is it right you can get a pig's heart? Just imagine that. When you die do you leave your body to medical science or Minshulls the local butcher? What do you think doctor?
	(The DOCTOR laughs politely.)
DOC	Now we must be serious for a moment. Try and think if there is anything I can help you with so that you have a better understanding of your condition.

BILLY	Well there is one thing I can't get my head round.
DOC	And that is?
BILLY	Why do they always wake me up at about half-eleven to give me a sleeping pill?
DOC	That is one of the unknown mysteries of the national health service I'm afraid. *(BILLY laughs. SARAH enters and overhears BILLY.)*
BILLY	But for all the good those sleeping tablets do me they may as well stick them up my arse.
SARAH	Now there's a big improvement! He said 'arse' beautifully doctor. He's definitely on the way, don't you think?
DOC	Compared to many I suppose I must have to say yes.
BILLY	I tell you what doctor. You're not at all like a real doctor.
DOC	And what is a real doctor supposed to be like Billy?
BILLY	You make me laugh.
DOC	And you know what they say don't you? Laughter is the best medicine...
	(MUSIC. LIGHTS fade to black. MUSIC continues until LIGHTS come up. BILLY is standing with his coat on. LIZ is holding a small suitcase. SARAH is standing there with a wheelchair and a blanket. ALBERT, SANDRA and HILDA come shuffling in.)
BILLY	*(to SARAH)* Can't I walk out properly by myself? Or at least try to?
SARAH	Sorry Billy. It's a definite No, No. Rules and all that. What if you fall? You could end up in hospital. You can say your goodbyes in here. Ok? But we do have to wheel you out. If

you go arse about face it just means more paperwork.

LIZ   *(to BILLY)* She's caught that from you. I suppose everybody in here is saying 'arse' now. And *you* need a foot up your arse. My God, I'm at it now.

(BILLY hobbles to the other patients saying goodbyes and hugging and shaking hands. Right hands only, of course.)

BILLY   Bye, Sandra. Take care of yourself.

SANDRA   I will, dear. Send me an invite to your wedding, wont you?

LIZ   *(dryly)* I have to get an invite to it *myself* first!

BILLY   *(moving on to HILDA)* Bye, Hilda. Don't do anything I wouldn't do.

HILDA   Oh blimey! Don't put restrictions on me. I'm an adventurous woman!

BILLY   You're a bloody menace! If ever anyone needs bromide in their tea, it's you. Bye love. *(He kisses her cheek, moves to ALBERT).* Bye Albert, you miserable old git. I shall miss you.

ALBERT   *(pretending not to care)* Garn! I'll be glad to see the back of you, meself.

(BILLY then goes very quiet and stands very still. He is close to tears and trying to hide it. LIZ notices and takes his arm and leads him to his wheelchair.)

LIZ   Your carriage awaits, my Lord. Here I'll put this blanket around you. We don't want you catching cold.

SARAH   That's right. You tell him, Liz. Paperwork! If he gets a cold now, it's more paperwork.

(SARAH begins to help to tuck BILLY in. BILLY then puts one arm around her and begins to sob. Everyone looks

uncomfortable.)

SARAH   *(To LIZ)* Don't worry love. It happens a lot when they leave.
           They've formed an attachment to what they feel is a safe
           place. It'll take time but it should become easier by the day.

BILLY   I'm really going to miss everyone. Especially you Sarah.
           Nobody has given me so much attention. Not even my Liz.

LIZ   Oh, thank you!

BILLY   I don't know how I'll manage without you.

SARAH   Of course you'll manage, Billy. You are just suffering from
           P.A.T.

BILLY   P.A.T?

SARAH   Post Albert Trauma.

           (BILLY gives half a smile through his tears.)

BILLY   I'm scared. Why am I suddenly so frightened?

SARAH   There's nothing to be scared of. People leave us all the time.
           (to LIZ) This is a classic reaction. Patients leave their
           comfort zone and it can affect them quite badly. You will
           probably find that he starts to cry for no reason, and this
           can be triggered by many things.

LIZ   So what can I do to help him then?

SARAH   Simple! Bring him back to visit us! Oh… and don't let him
           watch 'Little House on the Prairie'. Not just yet anyway.

BILLY   I'm going to write a book about all this.

SARAH   That'll be good. A nice project for you to get your teeth into.

BILLY   No I am. Really. A funny book. About Albert and Hilda and
           Sandra and everything. I will.

LIZ	'Course you will, love. Right after we get married and have our first child…
BILLY	Bloody hell, you never give up, do you?
	(MUSIC. LIGHTS fade to black. MUSIC continues until LIGHTS come up again. VOICES are heard in the dark, microphoned and randomly saying:)
VOICE 1	Come on Billy! Get those fingers moving!
VOICE 2	I will write a book…
VOICE 3	Albert, you're disgraceful!
VOICE 5	What time do you call this?...*(again)* What time do you call this?
	(The LIGHTS come up to show BILLY slumped over the kitchen table, as in the beginning of the play. LIZ has her hand on the light switch. They are both in their dressing gowns. The kitchen is as it was at the beginning of the play.)
LIZ	*(annoyed)* I said what time do you call this, Billy?
	(BILLY suddenly jolts awake and stares at her.)
BILLY	*(confused)* I don't know off hand…what time is it?
LIZ	It is precisely five a.m. I know that because the digital display on the alarm clock told me. What are you doing down here at this time?
BILLY	I couldn't sleep, I was nervous.
LIZ	But you were asleep. Dead to the world on the kitchen table. It gave me a turn for a minute. I thought you'd…well… never mind.
BILLY	*(holding his hand up to his neck and flexing it in pain)* Yeah. I must have dozed off again. … Oh, it's all just nerves.

LIZ   What have you got to be nervous about?

BILLY   Have you forgotten what day it is?

LIZ   It's my day off – I know that much...

BILLY   And you know what date it is don't you?

LIZ   It's the...

BILLY   It's the first of April and you know what day that that is.
               Come on...you must!

LIZ   *(Clapping her hand to her mouth)* Oh my God! Yes of
               course! Your book comes out today! *(She bustles about
               getting cups and other stuff)* God! Fancy me forgetting! And
               I was so much a part of it, too! You have to admit. I have
               come up with the right title, don't you think? I mean, Green
               Tea wasn't going to work was it? No Never. 'Why I
               wouldn't go to war with Albert' ... nobody else would
               understand. 'At the stroke of six' wasn't bad. I know it was
               six o' clock when it happened but it's just not sexy is it? No!
               I have definitely chosen the right one.

BILLY   Yep. Today, 'A Stroke Of Luck' hits the bookshelves and I
               am, finally, a writer!

LIZ   *(putting a cup of tea in front of him and giving him a
               cuddle)* So, now, you'll be able to be a husband and daddy
               too, won't you?

BILLY   *(looking at her in amused disbelief)* Jesus! You never bloody
               give up, woman, do you?

BLACKOUT. MUSIC.

THE END

FURNITURE LIST

The Kitchen (SEE SET PLANS) small run of kitchen cupboards below a worktop (note that a sink is not necessary); 'back wall' above the worktop with a fake 'window' with drawn curtains. Light switch on wall. Track with floor length curtains. Small kitchen table with two chairs. Small computer station with one office chair or stool.

The Hospital Four high-backed hospital chairs (or wheelchairs) (one chair needs to have a raised footrest or a separate footrest); three of the chairs have adjustable side tables on casters; one wooden or plastic chair set against the curtains; one low TV table with TV on it (or TV with integral stand); drip on stand with bag of medication attached and a line to attach to BILLY.

PROPERTY LIST

ON STAGE	On kitchen worktop is a working electric kettle; two mugs; a caddy for teabags; a box of green tea, a bag or large bowl of sugar; several spoons; a non-working electric toaster; two PG Tips monkeys; packet of cigarettes and a lighter.
	On the kitchen table is a sheet of paper with instructions; an envelope containing a letter; a mobile phone. By the side of the kitchen table is an overnight bag or case with several items in (SEE PAGE 5 OF SCRIPT).
	On computer workstation is a laptop and an ashtray.
PAGE 5	LIZ exits and re-enters with letter.
PAGE 8	LIZ talks on her mobile phone.
PAGE 14	POLICEMAN enters with a battering ram.
PAGE 15	REMOVE kitchen table and chairs, computer workstation and ashtray. Draw curtains across kitchen.
	REPLACE with four hospital chairs or wheelchairs; three side tables; TV on table or integral stand.
	Drip attached to BILLY's arm, pillows behind him, blanket over him.
PAGE 18	LIZ enters with a shopping bag containing the toy monkeys and a comb.
PAGE 23	SARAH enters with a trolley which has three plates of food on it, covered with metal food covers, and also cutlery.
PAGE 25	REMOVE plates/food/cutlery/trolley/LIZ's chair/monkeys/drip on stand.
	REPLACE with TV Guide and remote control.
PAGE 31	SARAH enters with bingo cards and pencils/pens.
	SANDRA has her own pencil.

PAGE 36   BILLY has a coat/jacket on. LIZ is holding a small
               suitcase/bag. SARAH has a wheelchair and a blanket.

PAGE 40   LIZ needs two mugs.

LIGHTING AND EFFECTS PLOT

START	*MUSIC, LIGHTS – semi-darkness.*
PAGE 1	Cue: BILLY: Sorry, did I wake you?
	LIZ switches light on.
PAGE 7	Cue: *LIZ kisses BILLY on top of his head then exits, clutching the letter, his overnight bag and her cup of tea, and we see him sleeping but very restless.*
	LIGHTS go down.
PAGE 8	Cue: *LIZ appears downstage in a spotlight.*
	LIGHTS: spotlight on. Rest of stage black.
	Cue: LIZ: It was exactly twelve months to the day.
	LIGHTS: Spotlight fades. MUSIC. Allow time for BILLY to change clothes before bringing LIGHTS up and fading music.
PAGE 12	Cue: *BILLY: He dials 999.*
	SFX: telephone ringing. 999 voice (microphoned) (continues to p.14)
PAGE 14	Cue: BOB: She can give it too.
	SFX: Ambulance siren, getting louder, sound of vehicle stopping and doors slamming.
	Cue: BILLY: In here! In here!
	SFX: Commotion. Banging on front door.
	Cue: PARAMEDIC; The door won't open, sir.
	SFX: Another siren, getting louder, sound of vehicle stopping and doors slamming.
	Cue: PARAMEDIC: ...they are going to break the door down!
	SFX: battering ram and door splintering.

PAGE 15   Cue: BILLY: ...he's come as a bloody policeman!

LIGHTS: fade quickly to black.

MUSIC which continues until set has been changed and cast in place, then bring up LIGHTS and fade music.

PAGE 25   Cue: LIZ: Keep an eye on him, won't you girls?

LIGHTS: fade quickly to black.

MUSIC which continues until set has been changed and cast in place then fade music and bring up LIGHTS.

TV is blinking/hissing (optional).

PAGE 29   Cue: BILLY: It's called the Plumington Patient Poisoner.

LIGHTS: fade quickly to black.

MUSIC, which continues until cast in place then fade music and bring up LIGHTS.

PAGE 30   Cue: BILLY: ...and be prepared to be amazed...

LIGHTS: fade quickly to black.

MUSIC which continues until cast in place, then fade and bring LIGHTS up.

PAGE 31   Cue: SARAH: The consultant is coming to talk to you.

SFX: VOICE OF BINGO CALLER (microphoned)

PAGE 33   Cue: ALBERT: ...Elizabeth was wearing casual clothes.

SFX: VOICE OF BINGO CALLER (microphoned) (continues until p.35)

PAGE 35   Cue: HILDA: Are you any relation to Albert?

LIGHTS: fade quickly to black.

MUSIC which continues until cast in place then fades and bring LIGHTS up.

PAGE 36   Cue: DOCTOR: Laughter is the best medicine...

LIGHTS: fade quickly to black.

MUSIC which continues until cast in place then fades and bring LIGHTS up.

PAGE 39   Cue: BILLY: Bloody hell, you never give up do you?

LIGHTS: fade quickly to black.

SFX: MUSIC and voices (as per script) nightmare sequence.

MUSIC continues until set is changed and cast in place then fades and bring up LIGHTS.

PAGE 40   Cue: BILLY: You never bloody give up, woman, do you?

BLACKOUT. MUSIC. LIGHTS for curtain calls.

SET PLAN: THE KITCHEN SCENES

AERIAL VIEW

FRONT VIEW

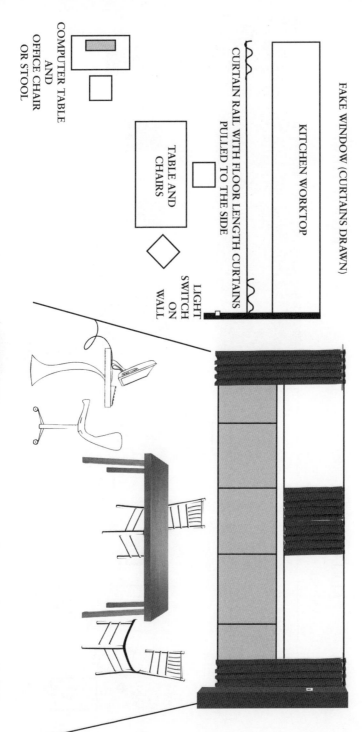

COMPUTER TABLE
AND
OFFICE CHAIR
OR STOOL.

CURTAIN RAIL WITH FLOOR LENGTH CURTAINS
PULLED TO THE SIDE

FAKE WINDOW (CURTAINS DRAWN)

KITCHEN WORKTOP

TABLE AND
CHAIRS

LIGHT
SWITCH
ON
WALL

AUDIENCE

SET PLAN: THE HOSPITAL SCENES

AERIAL VIEW

FRONT VIEW

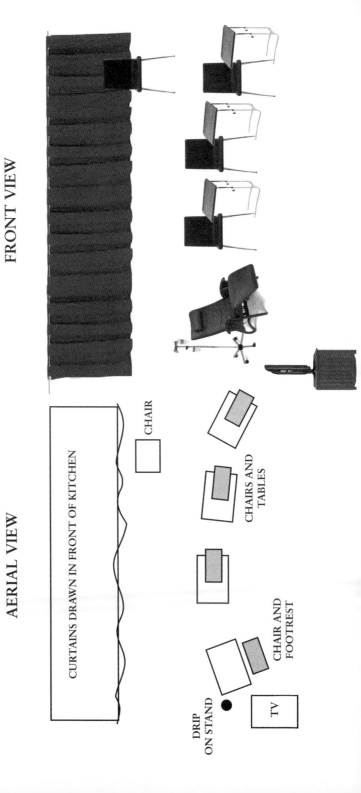

CURTAINS DRAWN IN FRONT OF KITCHEN

CHAIR

CHAIRS AND TABLES

CHAIR AND FOOTREST

DRIP ON STAND

TV